Melissa Boyd

Enjoy Kindness is Cool!
—DR BOYD

Kindness is Cool

Copyright © 2023 by Boyd Books

All rights reserved. This book or any portion thereof may not be reproduced or used in any manner whatsoever without the express written permission of the publisher except for the use of brief quotations in a book review.

Printed in the United States of America

First Edition, 2023

ISBN 978-1-955170-10-9 paperback

ISBN 978-1-955170-11-6 hardcover

This Book is dedicated to Bryanna, Bryan, & Bryson.
May you love kindness and walk humbly
with God.

Whether at home, the playground, or at school,
I've learned that showing kindness is really cool.

The more you practice kindness it will become easy for you.

Here are some examples of kind acts you can do.

Kindness is helping my little brother tie his shoe.

It is apologizing when I say something untrue.

It is cheering for my team, even when I don't score.

Kindness is saying caring words to a friend who is sad.

It is helping my sister calm down when she is really mad.

Kindness is not interrupting when I have something to say.

It is taking turns with a friend when we play.

Kindness is caring for my puppy when he does not feel well.

It is saying good job to a friend when they excel.

It is cleaning up my dinner plate and doing my chores.

Kindness is holding doors open when walking outside.

It's waiting my turn when playing with friends on a slide.

Kindness is letting my dad choose a game he wants to play.

It is having a good mood when I don't get my own way.

Kindness is surprising my mom with a homemade birthday card.

It is inviting a new neighbor over to play ball in the yard.

Kindness is sharing an umbrella in the pouring rain.

It is helping a older person walking with a cane.

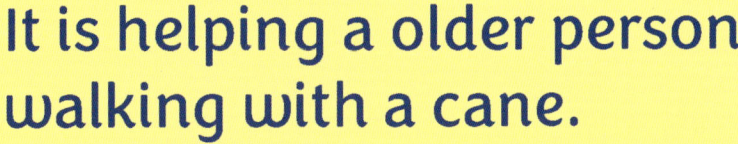

Kindness is listening to your sister when she has a lot to say.

It is cleaning up my toys at the end of the day.

Kindness is many things to include showing love to just you!

It is being caring, thoughtful, and proud of great things you do!

Encourage (Be Kind) to one another and build each other Up.

My Favorite Acts of Kindness are:

1._____

2._____

3._____

Be Sure to Check Out the Skills for Kids Book Series

 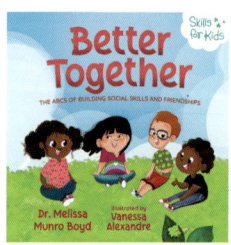   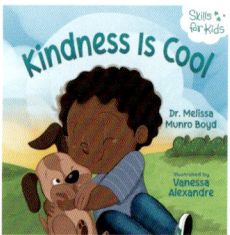

Instagram.com/author_melissaboyd
Facebook.com/melissamunroboydauthor
www.skillsforkidsbooks.com